Personal Application Workbook

for

Be Ye
Transformed

by
Nancy Missler

The King's *High* Way Ministries, Inc.

Be Ye Transformed Workbook

© Copyright 1996

Tenth Printing August, 2007

Published by The King's *High* Way Ministries, Inc.
P.O. Box 3111
Coeur d'Alene, ID 83816
www.kingshighway.org

ISBN 978-0-9745177-9-7

All Rights Reserved. No portion of this book may be reproduced in any form whatsoever without the written permission of the Publisher.

All Scripture quotations are from the King James Version of the Holy Bible.

PRINTED IN THE UNITED STATES OF AMERICA

Table of Contents

Introduction

Romans 12:1-2 exhorts us, "I beseech you brethren, by the mercies of God, that ye present your bodies a living sacrifice, holy, acceptable unto God, which is your reasonable service. And be not conformed to this world, but ***Be Ye Transformed*** by the renewing of your mind, [so] that ye may prove what is that good, and acceptable, and perfect will of God."

The dictionary says that a "transformer is an electric device that transforms energy from one circuit to another, with changed values of voltage." In the Christian vernacular, transformation simply means *an exchange of life*. It means taking off "self" and putting on God. Transformation is the goal and purpose of every Christian—to truly show forth Christ's Life in place of our own.

God's Will is that we be "conformed into His Image," and not simply conformed to the world's image. The above Scripture tells us, however, that the only way that this transformation occurs is by the constant *renewing of our minds*. The *Be Ye Transformed* Textbook and this Workbook are designed to help us understand the authority and power of God that we already possess in order to make this a reality in our own lives.

Purpose of the Workbook

The goal or purpose of this workbook is to stimulate you to apply the Scriptural principles presented in the *Be Ye Transformed* textbook to your life. True spiritual growth comes not from simply reading a book or attending a Bible study, but by the personal application of the material to your life.

This workbook is designed to help you learn how to *renew your mind* so that you <u>can</u> be *transformed into Christ's Image* as He desires. You will gain the maximum benefit from this workbook by reading a chapter in the *Be Ye Transformed* textbook and then completing the corresponding chapter workbook questions. You will quickly see how specific Scriptures apply to your own situation. You will receive deeper insights into God's character and His great Love for you. You will also begin to understand your own *natural reactions* a little more clearly and, at the same time, learn an alternative way of dealing with them.

It is our desire to help you intimately experience God's Love, Wisdom and Power in your daily life so you can have that "abundant life" He promises. "I am come that they might have *life*, and that they might have it more abundantly." (John 10:10)

How To Use This Workbook

This *Personal Application Workbook* is designed to accompany the *Be Ye Transformed* textbook. You should have your own textbook and your own workbook. Each chapter in the workbook corresponds to the same chapter in *Be Ye Transformed* textbook. The questions in the workbook should be completed *after* the corresponding chapter in the textbook has been read.

The workbook questions are divided into three categories: **Group Discussion Questions**, **Personal Questions**, and **Continue at Home Questions**.

- If you will be using this study for **personal Bible study**, it is suggested that you do all the workbook questions (Personal, Group, and At Home).

- If this study is to be used by **small discussion groups**, it is suggested that the leader of the group use the Group Discussion Questions and whatever Personal Questions are applicable. Continue at Home projects can be used during the week. (See the *Role of the Discussion Leader* at the end of this workbook.)

- Finally, if this study is to be used for a **large, corporate group** (where small discussion groups are not feasible), it is suggested that the appropriate questions be selected by the leadership and used for individual home study.

Personal Bible Study

Critical to any Bible study, whether it be personal or corporate, is prayer. Pray and ask God to search your heart and reveal anything that might hinder you from hearing Him. Then cleanse your heart of these things, so you can receive *all* that He has for you.

Along with your King James Bible, it is often helpful to have the following: a modern translation of the Bible (like the New American Standard Bible or the New International Version); a Bible Dictionary to look up any unfamiliar words, names and places; and a concordance (Strong's Concordance comes in a paperback form).

Read the appropriate chapter in the textbook. You must understand the principles and concepts of *Be Ye Transformed* textbook before you can really answer the questions properly and apply the principles to your life.

Look up all the Scriptures listed under each question. Meditate upon each one. It's the Word of God that will change your life, not a textbook or a class. Write out on 3x5 cards the Scriptures that particularly minister to you. Look up the important words in the original Hebrew or Greek, using your Strong's Concordance. Then you can be sure you are getting the *real* meaning of each word. So often the English translation in the Bible is far from what the original word meant.

Write out your answers in the space provided under each question. If you need more space, there are additional blank pages at the end of this workbook.

It's important to keep a personal journal. Write down all your experiences with God. Note the promises He gives you from Scripture, as well as the experiences He allows in your life. Express your real feelings and emotions about these things—no one should ever see your journal but you. Most importantly, write down the things that you give over to God as you cleanse your heart each day.

What a blessing and an encouragement this journal will be when you read it later on. In those times when you are going through a "valley," your entries in the journal will remind you of all that God has done for you and of His complete faithfulness to perform His promises. Your journal will give you the encouragement and the *hope* to make the same faith choices again.

Group Bible Study

This workbook, along with the *Be Ye Transformed* textbook, can also be used for small group discussions. Learning takes place through the understanding and sharing of Biblical principles with intimate friends, such as in a small discussion group. A discussion group of about eight to ten people is ideal, and each of these groups should have a leader to guide the sharing. The *Role of the Discussion Leader* is explored in detail at the end of this workbook.

The first thing to do in all Bible studies is to pray. Prayer is what changes things—our hearts, our attitude, our situation, other people, etc. Pray continually.

Always come to the study prepared, having first read the entire chapter in the textbook, then having completed the appropriate questions in the workbook.

Look up all the Scriptures listed under each question. Meditate upon each one. It's the Word of God that will change your life, not a textbook or a class. Write out on 3x5 cards the Scriptures that particularly ministered to you.

Look up in your Strong's Concordance the important words in the original Hebrew or Greek. Then you can be confident of the true meaning of the words.

Be willing to join in the discussions. If you have completed the questions and have some understanding of the chapter, you will feel comfortable in sharing. The leader of the group is not there to lecture, but to encourage others to share what they have learned.

Have your answers applicable to the chapter in discussion. Keep the discussion centered upon the principles presented in the *Be Ye Transformed* textbook, rather than on what you have "heard" others say or on what you have "read" elsewhere. Keep focused.

Be sensitive to the other members of the group. Listen when they speak and be encouraging to them. This will prompt more people to share.

Do not dominate the discussion. Participate, but remember that others need to have equal time.

If you are a discussion leader, suggested answers, additional suggestions, and helpful ideas are in the *Be Ye Transformed Leader's Guide*. Also, see the "Role of the Discussion Leader" section at the end of this workbook.

Above all, pray for God's guidance and grace to love Him as He desires and be that open vessel to pass along His Love.

* * * * *

"*Search the Scriptures*; for in them ye think ye have eternal life: and they are they which testify of Me." (John 5:39, emphasis added)

Chapter 1: How Do Our Lives Become Transformed?

Overview

3 John 4 says, "I have no greater joy than to hear my children walk in truth."

"Walking in truth" is God's Will for all of us. If we *say* with our words that we are Christians, then it truly must be Jesus' Life that is shown forth from our lives. Scripture tells us that this is the whole purpose for our being called as Christians. God wants us *living His Love, reflecting His Thoughts and operating under His Power*. This is what Romans 8:28-29 means when it says we are to be "conformed into the Image of Jesus Christ."

Unfortunately, this "transformation" does not happen automatically. The only way we can make sure it's Christ's Life that is showing forth from our lives and not our own is by constantly *renewing our minds*. Transformation simply means *exchanging lives with Christ*. We give Him ours; He gives us His. When we don't know how to do this, however, we go on depending upon our own thinking, and God's Life in our hearts gets quenched.

God has given us the Mind of Christ in order to help us get His Life from our hearts out into our lives. However, because of ignorance, not only as to what the Mind of Christ is, but also what it does and how it works, we end up being conformed to the world, living a lie and playing right into the enemy's hands.

Group Discussion Questions

1. As Christians, why is it so important that our *actions* match our *words*? (John 3:21; 7:18; 13:35; 1 John 1:5-7; 2:6; 3:18; Ephesians 5:8)

2. What is the definition of truth? (Jeremiah 1:12; John 1:14; 14:6; 1 John 3:18) Why is God's Word and His Spirit called Truth? (Isaiah 46:11c; John 6:63; Genesis 1:3)

3. Describe *self-life* and how it differs from God's Life. (Colossians 1:27; Galatians 2:20)

4. The Bible speaks so much about having "abundant life." What is it and why is it so important? (John 10:10; Galatians 2:20)

5. What is meant by the term "the exchanged life" or the "transformed life"? (John 12:24-25; 13:35; Ephesians 3:16; Romans 8:29; 1 John 4:12, 17; Galatians 4:19; 2 Corinthians 3:18)

6. Why is it so important to exchange lives with God? (Philippians 1:21; Colossians 1:27; Luke 11:33-34)

7. What is the *only* way we will be able to "live the truth"? (Romans 12:1-2; 2 Corinthians 4:11-12)

8. Why is a *renewed mind* the link to this transformation? (Ephesians 4:22-24)

9. What does Scripture tell us that our basic goal and purpose is as Christians? Does this happen automatically? Why/ why not? (1 Timothy 1:5; Romans 8: 28-29; 2 Corinthians 3:18; Philippians 1:20-21; Galatians 2:20; John 13:34-35; Ephesians 5:17-18; 1 John 4:16)

10. Why is Satan so intent upon keeping us ignorant as to *how* to renew our minds? (Luke 11:33-36)

11. 1 Corinthians 2:16 tells us that if we are "born again," we have the Mind of Christ. Why then, do we continue to depend upon our own thinking and not God's?

12. Our own *thoughts* are critical to God. Why? Describe the "chain-reaction" of our souls. (2 Corinthians 10:5; James 1:14-15)

Personal Questions

1. What key points in this chapter stood out to you, and/or have affected your life the most? Do any of you have something you want to share?

2. Have you or are you experiencing any situations or struggles similar to those that were shared in this Chapter? If so, what situations? What do you think God is trying to teach you through this study?

3. Is there an example in your life of how you were able to apply this teaching? If so, in what ways?

4. What kind of Jesus do you show to the world around you?

5.   What is <u>your</u> basic goal as a Christian? Have you been able to live up to it?

6.   What does "living the truth" personally, mean to you? In what areas of your life do you feel that you are <u>not</u> "living the truth"?

7.   Have you had situations in your life where you experienced "your thinking" completely different than "God's thinking"? What was the result?

8.   What does a *transformed life* personally mean to you? Do you see your own life being transformed? In what ways?

Continue at Home

1.   Write on a note card any Scriptures that particularly ministered to you in this chapter. Use them to help you apply these principles. Carry them with you or post them where you can see them as a constant reminder.

2.   Which of the following tend to motivate or control your actions the most? Circle the ones that apply to you:

3.   Fears, hurts, doubts, anger, pride, bitterness, resentment, insecurities, negative thoughts, others_____ .

4.   Begin to recognize the above things in your thinking this week; acknowledge your real feelings; tell God that you don't want to follow this way of thinking any more; give those negative thoughts over to God; and then, read His Word and begin to put the "Truth" back in where the lies have been.

MEMORIZE:
Roman 12:1-2
Galatians 2:20
John 10:10
Colossians 1:27
Philippians 1:21

READ:
2 Corinthians 4:10-11
John 12:24-25

Chapter 2: Mind Renewal

Overview

Renewing our minds is not simply "changing our thoughts" as the world does, but it's actually *putting off* our old negative thoughts, as well as *putting on* God's Thoughts.

One reason our "mind renewal" is so important to God is that He wants us to see all things that happen to us from His perspective and not from our own hurt and negative feelings. How hard this is, especially when we are going through trials. But, how important it is (especially in trials) to stay a genuine and true witness of Christ. The witness people remember the most is not what we "say," but what we "do!" Do we still show forth Christ, even in the hard times?

Another reason mind renewal is so important is *whoever controls our thinking controls our lives*. If Satan can influence our thinking by keeping us immersed in our own natural, emotional way of responding, he's got us and he doesn't have to do anything else. Truly, the battle is for our minds.

A third reason mind renewal is so important is that if there is no mind change, then there will be no life change either. Without a renewed mind, our lives will always remain the same, no matter what we do or try.

Finally, mind renewal is important because it's the only way we can discern the true from the false. We are not to judge or discern by our own eyes, but by the Mind of Christ. "...he shall not judge after the sight of his eyes, neither reprove after the hearing of his ears, but with righteousness shall he judge..." (Isaiah 11: 3-4)

Group Discussion Questions

1. In your own words, describe what exactly "mind renewal" is. What two things are involved? (Ephesians 4:22-24; Matthew 16:24; Colossians 1:27)

2. What are some of the reasons why "mind renewal" is so important? (Genesis 50:20; Proverbs 23:7; Jeremiah 48:11; 2 Corinthians 11:13-15; Luke 4:18; Romans 7:25b)

3. Do you think Joseph in the Old Testament (when he was in prison) knew that God was using him "to work all things together for good"? (Genesis 39:2, 4; 50:20) How do you see the trials that God has allowed in your life right now?

4. Why does Satan revel when we don't take our negative thoughts captive? (Proverbs 23:7; Matthew 6:23; 1 John 1:5-8)

5. Why does God use the eagle as a symbol of this "renewal process"? (Psalm 103:5)

6. Why is it true that if we have no mind change, we'll have no life change either? Can't we just memorize more Scriptures, go to more Bible studies and pray harder in order to have our lives change? Why/ why not? (Jeremiah 48:11; Psalm 51:6)

7. In the Old Testament, Isaiah says, "your iniquities have *separated* you and your God." In the New Testament, what do we mean when we say "things that are not of faith" (that we hold on to) *separate* us from God? (Isaiah 59:2; Psalm 119:70)

8. Why does God allow hurtful and painful situations into our lives? (Jeremiah 1:10; Job 16:12; 42:5)

9. What is God's purpose for suffering? (2 Corinthians 4:10-12)

Personal Questions

1. What key points stood out to you or have affected your life the most in this chapter and why?

2. Have you or are you experiencing any situations or struggles similar to those that were shared in this chapter. If so, what situations?

3. Are there any areas in your life right now where you know God wants you to apply this teaching? What areas?

4. Have you ever tried to make a "life change" without changing your thinking? What happened?

5. Has God ever allowed situations into your life that were hurtful or painful, but you knew He was using them to show you your wrong priorities and dependencies? Did you learn through these experiences to depend more upon Him and trust Him more?

6. Have you ever experienced that "separation," that "barrier" or that quenching of God's Spirit within you (that we have been talking about), but you didn't understand what was happening or how to correct it? What was the result?

7. What does "mind renewal" mean to you personally? Why do you feel this is so very important?

8. Has God brought "mind renewal" about in certain areas of your own life? Share specific situations.

Continue at Home

1. Write on a note card any Scriptures that particularly ministered to you in this chapter and use them to help you apply these principles. Memorize them.

2. This week, talk to God about improving the quality of your daily quiet time. Schedule a specific time with Him. Write out some of your prayers to Him. Use a daily reading guide to help you be consistent with your Bible reading.

3. Ask God to show you the areas that you are still not willing to lay down to Him. (You might not even be aware of them.) An attitude of "willingness" is so very critical; ask God to show you where you are falling short.

4. Begin a journal. Write down all the experiences God allows in your life this week—things that you need to "deal with" (attitudes you had, situations you didn't handle properly, people who bothered you, wrong responses you had, etc.). Describe your own thoughts and emotions about each situation.

Confess anything on your part that was "not of faith" and *repent* of it. *Give those things to God* and then, *read His Word* and replace those ungodly things with the truth.

MEMORIZE:

2 Corinthians 10:5
Ephesians 4:22-24
Romans 8:28
Jeremiah 29:11
Isaiah 40:31

READ:

James 1:22-24
Ephesians 3:16-19
Hosea 4:1
Isaiah 11:3-4
2 Corinthians 4:7-12

Chapter 3: What is Our Mind?

Overview

What is our mind? We will not be able to "renew our minds" unless we understand exactly what they are.

There is a lot of confusion, even in Christian circles, as to what our minds really are and what they do. Our minds are not just our brain, our reason or our intellect, but a whole conceptual process that begins with our spirit and ends with our life actions. In Scripture there are three types of minds. *Mind* in the natural man is a self-centered conceptual process. For this person there is no other choice because there is no other power source to produce anything different than what he thinks, feels or desires.

Mind in a believer, however, can be one of two kinds: either they can be a single-minded person or a double-minded person. Single-mindedness refers to a believer who has made the proper faith choices to allow God's Life from his heart to be manifested out in his soul. This is a person who is living *one life*. Jesus' Life is freely flowing from this person's heart out into his life actions.

Double-mindedness refers to a believer who, even though he has God's Life in his heart, has chosen to follow what his own feelings and thoughts are telling him to do, rather than doing what God's Spirit is prompting. Therefore, God's Life is quenched and blocked from coming forth into this person's soul, and he is thus showing forth *self-life* rather than God's Life. This is a person who is living *two lives*: God's Life in his heart and his own self-life in his soul.

Without constantly "renewing our minds," we'll simply be conformed to the world, not transformed out of it! Therefore, double-mindedness is Satan's game plan. He loves it when our words and our deeds don't match (i.e., when we "live a lie"), because then the Gospel won't be passed on.

Group Discussion Questions

1. Why has there been so much confusion about the word *mind*? Who benefits from this confusion? (2 Corinthians 11:3)

2. In your own words, can you describe what our mind is? (1 Corinthians 2:16; Romans 12:2)

3. Name two or three words that are often used in the Old Testament to describe the word *mind*. (Psalm 7:9; Proverbs 20:27; Leviticus 4:9)

4. Describe the three different types of *minds*. (1 Corinthians 2:14; Luke 11:33-36)

5. Describe the difference between *single-mindedness* and *double-mindedness*.

6. How is it that we can be Christians all of our lives and yet, many of our family and close friends don't even know that we really are?

7. Romans 12:1-2 tells us that we are to be "transformed." What exactly does this mean, in contrast to being "conformed to the world"?

8. When we are double-minded we are forced to "live a lie." Why? (Isaiah 59:10; Luke 11:33-35)

9. Luke 11:33-36 describes both double-mindedness and single-mindedness. Explain how.

Personal Questions

1. What key points in this chapter stood out to you or affected your life the most? Why?

2. Have you or are you experiencing any situations or struggles similar to those that were shared in this chapter? If so, what situations?

3. Are there any areas in your own life right now where you can apply this teaching? If so, what areas?

4. What principles are you still having difficulty understanding or applying?

5. Have you ever "lived a lie"? Have you ever felt and known in your heart that "God was the answer," and yet, your life actions disproved it? Was Jesus' Light "hidden under a bushel" in your heart? Can you share the situation?

6. Do you see your life being *transformed* as God desires? Or, do you see your life being "conformed to the world"?

7. Do your friends and family know, and is it evident by your life, that you are a Christian? What kind of Jesus do you show to them?

8. What personally comes to your mind, when you think of "single-mindedness"? Or, "double-mindedness"? Can you think of examples in your life where you were each of these? Why does Satan want you to stay double-minded?

Continue at Home

1. Write on a note card any Scriptures that particularly ministered to you in this chapter and use them to help you apply these principles.

2. Spend quiet time this week recommitting every area of your life to God. Are there any areas that you are still struggling with? By faith (not feelings) write these down in your journal and give them to God.

3. This week, pray and ask God to make you aware of your own negative and self-centered thoughts and feelings. In your journal, write down what God shows you. Choose to take these thoughts captive; confess that you have "owned" them; turn around from following them; and, give them to God. Then replace them with a few of your own favorite Scriptures.

4. Daily, ask God to fill you with His Love and His Wisdom and Power. Allow these things to be the motivation for all your choices this week.

MEMORIZE: **READ:**
Philippians 1:21   Matthew 25:1-10
Ephesians 4:23   Luke 11:33-36
Proverbs 20:27
Psalm 18:28
1 Corinthians 6:17

Chapter 4: Satan's Ways to Keep Us Double-Minded

Overview

God wants us to be single-minded and to show forth His Life in our souls. He wants us to "live the truth." Satan's goal for us, however, is double-mindedness, so that we'll be forced to "live a lie" (our words and our deeds don't match) and God's Life will be hidden from the world.

Satan has three primary ways he tries to keep us double-minded. First of all, he tries to make us disobedient to God's Word by not "taking every thought captive" and instead being consumed in our own negative thoughts and emotions. God's Word says that we are to have a readiness to "revenge all disobedience." In other words, we are to *deal with* anything that is "not of faith."

Satan, however, is determined to stir our feelings up so we will be hardened to hearing or doing God's Word. If this doesn't work, then he tries to get us to doubt God's Power to perform His Word in our lives. In other words, he wants to make us think that God is not faithful. This is why it's so critical that our confidence and our trust not be in what our fears or doubts are telling us, but only in what God says in His Word He will do.

The final way Satan tries to keep us double-minded is through our *pride*. Pride occurs when we become so hardened to hearing or doing God's Word that, instead, we totally give ourselves over to what we think, feel and desire. What we are saying to God at this time is, "what I want and feel" is more important than "what You desire." It's simply putting ourselves above God. It's loving (*agapao*) ourselves first and not God.

Satan is after our faith itself. If he can just get us to be disobedient, unbelieving and unwilling to follow God at all, he's got us and he doesn't have to do anything else. This choice is one that we all will constantly face—God's way or our own way.

Group Discussion Questions

1. Why does Satan rejoice when we are double-minded? Name some of the results of double-mindedness that he is after in each one of us. (Luke 11:34; James 1:8; Ezekiel 8:12; Luke 11:17)

2. What are Satan's three tactics to keep us double-minded? Explain each. (Genesis 3:1-7)

3. From the above question, we can understand the three primary means Satan uses to keep us double-minded. Can you recall some of the other places in Scripture that these same three tactics of his appear? (Jeremiah 13:10; Matthew 4:1-10; 1 John 2:16)

4. Why is it so easy for Satan to get us to disobey God's Word? (2 Corinthians 10:5-6)

5. If Satan tries to get us to disobey God's Word and it doesn't work, what is the next tactic he uses?

6. What does the "shield of faith" have to do with trusting God? (Ephesians 6:16)

7. There are many definitions for "pride." What is the one that means the most to you? (Isaiah 14:13-14)

8. As believers, what is the one continual choice that we all face (and we will continue to face until we see Jesus)? (Deuteronomy 30:15-18; Matthew 4:4-10; Ephesians 5:29)

Personal Questions

1. What key points of this chapter stood out to you or have affected your life the most? Why?

2. Is there an area in your life right now where you can apply this teaching? If so, can you share?

3. What principles in this chapter are you still having difficulty understanding or applying in your daily life?

4. Have you ever experienced the three tactics of Satan to keep you double-minded? What are some of the specific ways in your own life that he tries?

5. It is easy for Satan to get you to be consumed in your own thoughts and emotions and to disobey God's Word? Explain.

6. Have you been more aware of your moment-by-moment choices this week? How has this affected your life?

7. In the past, have you ever looked to others, positions or things to meet your needs for love and security? Share how.

Continue at Home

1. Write on a note card some of the Scriptures that particularly ministered to you in this chapter. Use them to help you apply these principles.

2. Ask God to help you be more aware of "double-mindedness" in your life this week. The next time He shows you something that is "not of faith," choose to set your own understanding and feelings aside, and trust and act upon what God has promised you in His word. It's imperative to stay single-minded so that God's Life can be passed on.

3. What things are you aware of in your own life that tend to quench God's Spirit in you? Ask Him to point these out to you this week and choose to give them over to Him so you can be rid of them for good.

4. Be sure to keep up your journal and quality quiet time before the Lord this week.

MEMORIZE: **READ:**
2 Corinthians 10:5-6   Deuteronomy 30:15-18
Romans 4:20-21; 14:23   James 1:5-7

Chapter 5: The Mind of Christ
(Part 1)

Overview

1. The Mind of Christ is a "divine" conceptual process. It's God's Holy Spirit that creates God's supernatural Thoughts in our hearts and through a process (again by the Holy Spirit) produces those Thoughts as Godly actions in our lives.

2. Isaiah 11:1-2 explains this divine process: God's Holy Spirit not only give us all of *God's Thoughts* (His Word), but He also gives us *understanding* of those thoughts; *counsel* as to which one of those thoughts are appropriate for our situation; His *strength* to implement those thoughts in our lives; *personal experiential knowledge* of seeing those thoughts manifested in our life actions; and finally, the ability to walk in the *fear of God* and not in the fear of man.

3. In Scripture, the Spirit of God is often spoken of as an eternal fountain of water springing up from within us. As we learn to set our self-life aside, God's Spirit can freely come forth from the innermost part of our being and fill our souls. God calls this the "fullness of God" and "abundant life."

4. Being filled with the "fullness of God" is what we are talking about here with the Mind of Christ. It's a continual re-filling and overflowing of God's Spirit in a cleansed and empty vessel. "And to know the Love of Christ, which passeth knowledge, that ye might be filled with all the fullness of God." (Ephesians 3:19)

Group Discussion Questions

1. In your own words, what is the Mind of Christ? Can you define it Scripturally? (Isaiah 11:1-2)

2. What is the main purpose of the Mind of Christ in us? (1 Corinthians 2:12-16; Isaiah 11:3-4; 1 Timothy 1:5)

3. The seven-fold Spirit of God is what gives us the Mind of Christ. What are some other illustrations that are used in Scripture to describe God's seven-fold Spirit? (Zechariah 4:2; Daniel 10:6; Luke 8:16; Psalm 32:8; Revelation 4:5)

4. In your own words, define exactly what the purpose of the Spirit of the Lord is in us. (1 Corinthians 6:17; 15:45; John 6:63; Romans 5:5)

5. In just a few words, can you describe the ministry of the Holy Spirit? (Acts 19:4; Psalm 18:28; Acts 19:6; Ephesians 5:18)

6. In your own words, what makes the continual *refilling* of the Holy Spirit so unique and so special? Why is it any different than the first three "gifts" of the Holy Spirit (the Holy Spirit "with us," "in us," and "upon us")? (Ephesians 3:19; John 4:14)

7. How are we daily filled with the Spirit? Is it from the *outside of us* inward or is it from *inside of us* outward? Is this a new concept for you? What are some other "terms" for this continual filling? (Ephesians 3:19; Isaiah 11:2; John 4:10-11; Luke 12:35)

8. In your own terms, define the Spirit of Wisdom. (Hebrews 8:10; Proverbs 4:4; Colossians 3:16; 1 Corinthians 2:7a)

9. Can this type of wisdom be studied for or bought? (Job 28:12-21; 1 Corinthians 1:19; 2:7-9)

10. Why does Scripture put such emphasis on having God's Wisdom in our hearts? (Proverbs 8:12-14, 34-35; Proverbs 2:1-5)

11. If we lack wisdom, what does Scripture say to do? (James 1:5-7) How do you personally find God's Wisdom when you need it?

12. Scripture tells us to hide God's Word in our hearts. (Psalm 119:11) How do we do this?

Personal Questions

1. What key points of this chapter stood out to you or have affected your life the most? Why?

2. Have you or are you experiencing any situations or struggles similar to those that were shared in this chapter? If so, what situations?

3. Are there any areas in your life right now where you may be able to apply this teaching? What areas?

4. What type of wisdom have you built your "house" upon? Man's? God's? Your own? Share.

5. How have you personally hidden God's Word in your heart? What are some of the practical ways that you do this?

6. Personally, what do you think the "sign" is that someone has been filled with the Spirit?

7. Do you allow the Holy Spirit to refill you daily? What specifically does this mean to you?

8. Why do you think it's so important to have a consistent quiet time and to be in the Word daily? What could you do to improve the consistency of your daily quiet time?

Continue at Home

1. On a note card, write out the Scriptures that particularly ministered to you in this chapter. Use them to help you apply these principles.

2. This week ask God to personally show you why it's so important to have and to pass on His Love and His Wisdom. In your journal, write down the things God shows you. Be prepared to share.

3. Every day this week, make a special time to be with the Lord. Continue to ask Him how you might improve the quality of your quiet time with Him. Continue to write out your prayers to Him. Choose to give Him all your expectations, desires and emotional needs. Ask Him to meet these needs and give you His Life. Once you are a cleansed vessel, ask Him to help you put the interests of others above your own. Be aware of your changed attitudes.

4. Praise and worship God more this week.

MEMORIZE:
Isaiah 11:2
John 4:14
Romans 10:17
Ephesians 5:18

READ:
1 Corinthians 2:12-16
James 1:5-7
Ephesians 3:17-19
John 4:10-11

Chapter 6: The Mind of Christ
(Part 2)

Overview

The first function or operation of the Mind of Christ in us, produced by the Spirit of the Lord, is the *Spirit of Wisdom*—which is all of God's Thoughts. It's God's Word "inscribed" in our hearts.

The next function of the Mind of Christ in us is the *Spirit of Understanding*––which is God's supernatural revelations to His Word. This is where God "turns on the lights" for us. Just because we have God's Word in our hearts doesn't necessarily mean we will understand that wisdom. This is where we need God's supernatural enlightenment.

The next operation of the Mind of Christ in us is the *Spirit of Counsel*—which is God's personal instructions as to what His Will is for our lives. The secret here is that we must "wait" for His Counsel and His advice. Only God knows our true situation and only He knows the hearts of the people involved. We mustn't lose hope if God doesn't answer us right away or in the way that we hoped He would.

The next function of the Mind of Christ in us is the *Spirit of Strength*. This operation of the Holy Spirit must go alongside of God's Counsel. It wouldn't make much sense for us to know God's Will for our lives if we didn't have the power to carry it out.

It's always important that the Lord does both the *counseling* and the *empowering.* Why? Because then God is the One who will get the glory for everything. So, God's Spirit of Counsel and Strength is God's authority and God's power to *put off* the habits of the flesh and to *put on* Christ. Scripture tells us that only these are the true "overcomers."

Group Discussion Questions

1. In your own words, define what God's Spirit of Understanding is. Why is it so critical to have God's Understanding alongside of His Wisdom? (Hosea 4: 14d; Proverbs 2:1-5; 3:19; 4:7)

2. What would you say is one of the basic reasons why so many people are stumbling and falling in the Christian walk today? What causes this? (Hosea 4:14d)

3. What is God's Spirit of Counsel and why is it so important? (Jeremiah 42:3; Romans 8:27)

4. What is the secret to knowing what God's Will is for our lives? Why is this so hard? (Isaiah 40:31)

5. Why can't our psychologists, pastors and counselors give us the answers we need? Why do we often end up worse off in the end when we depend upon them? (Psalm 108:12-13; Isaiah 30:1)

6. What's the difference between psychology and Christianity?

7. How do you personally know God's Will for your life?

8. What are the four steps we must take, if we don't have time to wait for God's Counsel? (Proverbs 3:5-6)

9. What capability of the Holy Spirit goes hand in hand with the Spirit of Counsel? (Philippians 2:13; Jeremiah 1:12)

10. Why is it so important that God does both the *counseling* and the *performing*? (Jeremiah 9:23-24)

11. 2 Corinthians 12:9 says that God's Power is made perfect in weakness. What exactly does this mean?

12. God's Strength in the Greek is defined "power to rein in." What does this really mean? (Luke 21:19)

13. In your own words, what does it mean to be an "overcomer"? (1 John 5:4)

Personal Questions

1. What key points stood out to you in this chapter or have affected your life the most?

2. Can you give an example of where you followed your own thoughts instead of what God was prompting you to do? What happened as a result?

3.   Have there been times in the past, where you have sat down and read God's Word and yet, after you were through, you didn't remember a thing? What was it that was not operating?

4.   Can you think of an example where you were so "weak" and you knew you couldn't do what God required, but God did it through you anyway? Have you ever gotten impatient and gone ahead and performed God's Will in your own power and strength? What happened?

5.   In the past, have you ever experienced being completely ignorant to the true motivations of your heart and then were shocked when God revealed them to you? Can you share the situation?

6.   Have you ever thought about the differences between Christianity and psychology? Is this new to you? Do you agree with what was shared?

7.   7. Do you have a hard time "waiting" for God's Counsel? Are there any situations or decisions in your life right now where you need to seek God's Counsel? Why is it critical to wait only for His Counsel?

8.   Are there any situations in your life right now where you're having a difficult time understanding what God is doing and you can't see how God is going to work it all out? What can you choose to do in the mean time?

Continue at Home

1.   Write on a note card the Scriptures that particularly ministered to you in this chapter. Use them to help you apply these principles.

2.   This week as you read God's Word and look up Scriptures, ask God to illuminate your heart and give you new understanding of His Wisdom.

3.   Philippians 2:13 says that God is in us not only "to will," but also "to do." This week, continually pray for His Power to produce His Life in you. Share the situations He gives you to practice this.

4.   Write down specific questions that you need God's Counsel on. Pray about these, read the Word and expect God to answer.

MEMORIZE: **READ:**
Proverbs 4:7   Proverbs 2:1-5
Hebrews 4:12   Ephesians 4:22-24
Proverbs 3:5-6
Philippians 2:13
Zechariah 4:6
1 John 5:4

Chapter 7: The Mind of Christ
(Part 3)

Overview

God has given us His Wisdom, His Understanding, His Counsel and His Strength. Now, it's up to us whether we will choose to follow these things or not. Our "choices" turn out to be the critical "crossroads" of our lives. Our choices are what decide whose "life" will be lived in our souls, either God's or our own. We have the free choice to either follow what God has shown us and rely upon His ability to perform these things in our lives; or, we can choose to follow what our own self-centered thoughts and emotions are telling us and rely upon our own ability to implement these things in our lives.

The next two functions of the Mind of Christ in us are the *Spirit of Knowledge* and the *Fear of the Lord*. There is something very unique about these two capabilities: they are our own responsibility to achieve, moment by moment. Not only are we to make the right faith choices, but we are also to constantly lay down our lives so that God's Will can be performed through them.

We must remember that our self-life does not improve with age. We can be Christians for over 40 years and our self-life will still be just as ugly as it was the first day we believed. What does improve with age, however, is the ability to recognize our "self" and to choose to give it over to God. When we do this, we can be assured of intimate, first-hand knowledge of God's Life and of walking in the Fear of God, not the fear of man.

This is the "transformed life" that God desires for each one of us. This transformation is the climax of our relationship with God and the goal and purpose of our lives as Christians. When we walk in the Fear of God, it means that we are experiencing such an intimacy with God that we constantly will flee anything that would quench that oneness. Walking like this—in God's Love and Truth—is the result of the Mind of Christ operating fully in us.

Group Discussion Questions

1. Why is our *free choice* the critical crossroads of our lives? (Romans 6:6-7, 13; 7:25)

2.   Why do only Christians have a free choice decision? (Matthew 26:39)

3.   What is a "contrary choice"? (1 Corinthians 7:37; John 10:18)

4.   What makes *Knowledge of God* and *Fear of God* different from the other functions of the Mind of Christ in us? What two steps are required? (Romans 12:1-2; 2 Corinthians 4:10-12)

5.   What exactly is the Spirit of Knowledge?   Is this simply intellectual knowledge or head knowledge? Why/ why not?   (Galatians 2:20)

6.   Why is it that so few Christians never progress beyond "beginning knowledge" of God?

7.   What does *Fear of God* mean to you? Why must we intimately know Him *before* we can walk in this way? (Isaiah 11:3)

8.   Have we "arrived" when we learn to walk in the *Fear of God*?

9. What is the *transformation* that the Bible talks about? (Romans 12:1-2) Are we able to automatically stay transformed the longer we have been Christians? What is it that does improve with age? In light of this, define "maturity in Christ."

Personal Questions

1. What key points stood out to you in this chapter or have affected your life the most?

2. Have you or are you experiencing any situations or struggles similar to those that were shared in this chapter? If so, what situations?

3. Why is our choice the "key" to our Christian walk? Explain what a "faith" choice is. Do non-believers have this kind of a choice? Why/ why not?

4. Give an example of a situation this past month where you made a faith choice. What happened? Give an example of an emotional choice. What happened there?

5. Have you ever just stopped choosing God's way and gone back to where you started from as a Christian? What happened? Were you able to finally break through?

6. Do you really trust God in your life? Are you able to, without fear, lay your life down to Him because you know He loves you?

7. Do you walk in the "Fear of God" most of the time or in the fear of man? Be honest.

8. What does *intimate knowledge* of God mean to you? Is this kind of knowledge important to you to have? How well do you really know Jesus?

Continue at Home

1. Write on a note card the Scriptures that particularly ministered to you in this chapter. Use them to help you apply these principles.

2. Take a good, honest look at your life. Ask yourself, "Do I really have intimacy with God?" If you don't, ask yourself, "What am I going to do about it?" Hosea 4:16 says that "without intimacy (experiential knowledge of God) people will go into bondage." Are you going to settle for that? Talk to Jesus about it.

3. Ask yourself, "Am I willing to walk in an intimate, face to face, relationship with God no matter what others say, no matter how I feel or what I think and no matter how others treat me?" If your honest answer is "No," then ask Jesus to reveal to you why. Why are you afraid to lay everything down to Him?

MEMORIZE:
Galatians 2:20
2 Corinthians 4:10-11
1 Corinthians 2:2
1 Corinthians 6:19-20

READ:
Proverbs 1:1-5
Philippians 3:8-10
Colossians 3:12-14

Chapter 8: Blueprint of a Believer

Overview

In order for us to understand and see (visually) how the Mind of Christ works in us, we compare Solomon's Temple in the Old Testament to the internal architecture of man—spirit, heart, will and soul.

God uses "word pictures" in Scripture to help us understand His Word a little more clearly. One of these word pictures is 1 Corinthians 3:16 which says, "Know ye not that you are a *temple of God*, and that the Spirit of God dwells in you." Paul is making an analogy here by saying that our body is a temple and that this temple is now the dwelling place of the Holy Spirit. He is making a correlation between Solomon's Temple, which used to be the dwelling place of God, and our bodies that now are the dwelling place of God. He is saying that Solomon's Temple is a *blueprint of a believer indwelt by the Holy Spirit.*

The Jews believed the purpose for their temple was to glorify and to show forth *God's Name*, His Character and His Image. This is important because this is our own purpose as Christians—to show forth Christ's Life, His Image and His Name.

Thus, in order to understand ourselves better and how the Mind of Christ works in us, in this chapter we compare our bodies, as the temple of God now, to Solomon's Temple, which used to be the dwelling place of God. By doing so we get a better picture of what our spirit, heart, willpower, soul and body are. And thus, we can understand and see a little more clearly how the Mind of Christ fits into this whole picture.

Group Discussion Questions

1. Why do we compare the architecture of man to the Temple of Solomon in the Old Testament? What connection do they have with each other? (Hosea 12:10)

2. Why do we use Solomon's Temple as a model of man, and not Herod's Temple or Nehemiah's? (1 Chronicles 22:6-15; 28:11-13)

3.   What did the Jews believe that the purpose of the Temple was? How does this personally apply to us? (2 Samuel 7:13; 1 Kings 8:10-11, 16)

4.   As best you can, without looking at your book, name what all the rooms and courts of Solomon's Temple and what they correspond to in man:

       Holy of Holies   _____
       Holy Place   _____
       Porch   _____
       Hidden Chambers   _____
       Inner Court   _____
       Outer Court   _____

5.   As you look at the Temple chart, you can see that there are two very significant areas besides the Holy of Holies, the Holy Place and the Courtyards. What are they? What do they correspond to in us and what do they do?

Personal Questions

1.   What key points of this chapter stood out to you or have affected your life the most and why?

2.   Can you think of an area in your life where you might be able to apply this teaching? If so, in what ways?

3.   Have you ever seen a model of man that has helped you to understand yourself better? Was it Scriptural? What did you learn from it? Does studying Solomon's Temple help you to better understand yourself? In what ways?

4. The Jews believed their Temple was to show forth God and His Character (His Name). Is that your purpose as the temple of God? Have you ever thought about this before?

5. According to Scripture (and Chart 9), what are the three *"new"* things (areas) that each of us receive as a result of being "born again"?

6. Are there any principles in this chapter that you are still having difficulty understanding?

Continue at Home

1. Write on a note card all the Scriptures that particularly ministered to you in this chapter. Use them to help you apply these principles.

2. Go over the charts in this chapter every day this week. Become familiar with them. At the end of the week, take a piece of paper and, as best as you can, draw Solomon's Temple as a blueprint of yourself. Show where your heart, will and soul are. Define them on your paper as best you can.

3. Ask God to show you the times you begin to trust in your own ability to live the Christian life, rather than depending upon Him to produce His Life through you. Recognize these times and deal with you thoughts and emotions in the proper way. Be prepared to share examples.

4. Every day this week, make a special time to be with the Lord. Choose to give Him all your expectations, desires and emotional needs. Ask Him to meet these needs and give you His Life. Once you are a cleansed vessel, ask Him to help you put the interests of others (your spouse, your family, etc.) above your own.

MEMORIZE:
Matthew 22:37
1 Corinthians 6:20
Ezekiel 36:26
Romans 6:6-7

READ:
Malachi 1:11
2 Corinthians 6:16
Romans 5:17-18

Chapter 9: New Spirit, Heart and Will

Overview

In this chapter we explore, in greater detail, our spirit, heart and will and what each of their functions is. The *new spirit* that we receive as a result of being born again is a completely new power source or energy source. It's now God Himself dwelling in us. 1 Corinthians 6:17 tells us that (if we are born again) we have become *one spirit* with God.

Our *new heart* is the place where God's Life is created by God's Spirit. This new heart is not simply the old one changed or made new, but a totally new heart. In other words, when we are born-again, God replaces our old human heart with His brand-new heart filled with His supernatural Life: His Love, Wisdom and Power.

So the Life that is now in our hearts is totally pure and completely holy, because it's God's Life and not our own. All we need to learn, then, is how to let His Life flow from our hearts into our souls. This new heart is the center core of our whole being and upon this foundation everything else will be built. Again, God's Life in our hearts is likened to a "fountain of living water." When we say "yes" to God's Will, that living water gushes forth and fills us to overflowing. However, when we say "no" to God's promptings and make emotional choices to follow our own will and desires, God's Life gets blocked in our hearts, and that living water is not able to come forth.

Thus, it's our moment-by-moment choices that determine whose life will be lived in our souls—God's or our own. Our only responsibility is to make the appropriate faith choices; God then will align our feelings with the choices we have made and make us genuine.

Group Discussion Questions

1. In your own words, what is our new spirit? How does it differ from our human spirit? (Ezekiel 36:26)

2. Why is our heart such a significant area? (Colossians 1:9, 27)

3. Do you believe that we have a brand new heart after we are born again? Or, do you believe our heart is still evil and corrupt? (Genesis 8:21c)

4. Not only is our old, human heart evil and deceitful above all things, but what two other negative characteristics does it have according to Jeremiah 17:9?

5. If our hearts are made "new" when we are born again, then what is it that so desperately needs to be transformed? Why?

6. Explain why God's Spirit within us is often referred to as a "fountain of living water." (John 4:14; Jeremiah 17:13c) How does that fountain water become polluted? (James 3:10-11)

7. What part of man is the center core of his being and the base upon which everything else will be built? Why?

8. Why is our willpower (*dianoia*) the most critically important part of our makeup? What does *"dia"* and *"noia"* mean?

9. What are the two parts to our willpower? What does each part do?

10. The Bronze Pillars of the Temple porch, which represent our *free choice*, had names. What were they and why are they so significant to us?

11. We are programmed from youth "to feel" everything we choose. Is this still necessary as Christians? (Mark 9:24; Matthew 26:39)

12. If we don't have to "feel" our choices, what is our only responsibility? What is required next? Can we change our own feelings?

13. What are the two choices that we are constantly faced with? (Matthew 26:39)

Personal Questions

1. What key points of this chapter stood out to you or have affected your life the most and why?

2. Are you experiencing any situations similar to those that were shared in this chapter? If so, what situations?

3. Can real or lasting change occur before we are born again? Why/ why not? Did you ever try to change or improve yourself before you were born again? If so, what happened?

4. Personally, how does knowing that you have a brand, new heart (Christ's Life in you) affect everything you choose? Does it make a difference in your walk?

5. Is it a new concept for you that you don't have to "feel" your choices, but simply make them by faith? Do you have any examples of faith choices you made this week?

6. Many Christians still believe that our hearts are the place that stills needs to be transformed. Is it a new concept for you that the only "transforming" that needs to occur, is in our souls, our lives?

7. Does it help you in making your choices, to know that you have a supernatural willpower and that God, Himself, will *counsel* you as to what His Will is and then, give you the *strength* to perform it in your life? Share some examples.

8. When you make a "faith choice," whose life is lived in your soul? When you make an *emotional choice,* whose life is lived? Why does Satan love it when you make an *emotional choice*?

Continue at Home

1. Write on a note card all the Scriptures that particularly ministered to you in this chapter. Use them to help you apply these principles.

2. Ask God to make you aware of your choices this week. Ask Him to remind you when you should be making *faith choices.*

3. In Matthew 26:39, Jesus said, "Not my will, but thine." Write down some of your own thoughts and emotions that God has had you surrender to Him this week. Did you recognize right away that they were "not of faith"? Did you give them over to Him immediately? Did He change your feelings to match your choices? Be prepared to share.

MEMORIZE:
John 3:3
Jeremiah 31:3
Colossians 1:27
Ezekiel 11:19

READ:
1 Peter 3:4
Deuteronomy 30:19-20
Matthew 23:27

Chapter 10: Soul and Body

Overview

Our soul is like a "neutral area" that can either be filled with God's Life and moved powerfully and positively by God's Spirit; or, if His Spirit has been quenched by wrong choices, our soul will "wax cold" and be empty of meaning, because it will be filled with self-life and not God's Life at all.

Our souls are made up of our *conscious* thoughts, emotions and desires—our self-life. There is also a *subconscious* part of our soul—our hidden chambers. As believers, our souls can either show forth God's Life from our hearts and be single-minded (because one life is being lived); or, God's Life can become quenched and the soul life that is thus produced will be self-life or double-mindedness (because two lives are being lived).

Self-life is triggered by the hurts, resentments, pride and bitterness, etc. that we have never properly dealt with before (or given to God), but simply have stuffed down in our hidden chambers. God allows the *power of sin* access to these hidden chambers as a means by which He can expose what's down there. He wants us to "see" for ourselves the things that are "not of faith" so that we will choose to "deal with them" the proper way and be rid of them forever.

When we do it God's way, we not only are freed from the power of sin, but also we bind Satan from having any control over us in this area anymore. Thus, the war that constantly goes on within us is in our souls and not our hearts.

Group Discussion Questions

1. What is the two-fold root meaning for the Greek word, *psyche*? Why is this so significant?

2. Scripturally, what determines whether we are simply "in the Spirit" or whether we are "walking by the Spirit"? Can you elaborate on this? (Galatians 5: 25)

3. Again, what is the meaning and purpose of our Christian walk? (Ephesians 3:19; 2 Corinthians 2:14) Can anything else bring us this fulfillment and meaning? Why/ why not?

4. In your own words, describe what our soul is. What, then, is "our flesh"?

5. "Life" exists both in our souls and also in our hearts. Explain the difference between the two? (Proverbs 4:23) What is the *key* to having souls "like a watered garden"? (Jeremiah 31:12d)

6. From memory, can you draw what we look like, as the temple of God, when we make "faith choices" and are spirit-filled or single-minded? (Luke 11:33 d & e)

7. Now, draw the same temple. Only this time, draw what we look like when we make "emotional choices" that quench God's Spirit and that cause us to be double-minded. (Luke 11:33 b & c)

8. If we as believers already have God's Life in our hearts, where then, does our self-life come from? (Proverbs 5:22) What is this area called?

9. Can you explain what *sanctification* means and what it does? (1 Corinthians 5:7-8; 2 Corinthians 4:10-11)

10. Why is it impossible to separate our souls and our bodies?

11. How is it, we can be Christians all our lives, and yet no one knows it? Explain what "living a lie" means to you.

12. What is the *power of sin*? Where does it dwell, what does it do and what does it have access to? (Romans 7:20-21, 23)

13. What is it that can quench God's Power in us and open us up to the *power of sin*? What areas are "inviolate" to Satan and his *power of sin*?

14. Why are we "open prey" for the enemy when we *walk after the flesh*? (Romans 6:12, 16)

15. When we make *faith choices*, what are some of the results that we can expect? (Ephesians 3:19; Romans 6:7; 2 John 4; Philippians 1:21)

16. Where does the "war" between the *Power of God* and the *power of sin* take place? Why is this important to understand?

Personal Questions

1. What key points in this chapter stood out to you or have affected your life the most?

2. Have you experienced any situation or struggle similar to those that were shared in this chapter?

3. Before this study, how did you deal with your sin? Did you confess it and repent of it, or did you just "give it to God"? Did it ever seem to come back?

4. Have these temple models helped you to understand how we can be Christians with God's Life in our hearts, and yet still walk by the flesh? In what ways have they personally helped you?

5. Before this study, did you have a clear understanding of the difference between your "spirit" and your "heart"? Your "soul" and your "flesh"? How has understanding these things, helped you in your daily walk with God? What principles in this teaching are you still having difficulty understanding?

6. What is it that causes things to be stored in our hidden chambers in the first place? How do these hidden things affect our lives?

7. What are you enabling Satan to do every time you make an emotional choice?

8. Is there a situation in your own life right now where you feel "justified" in holding on to your own negative thoughts and emotions? What happens when you choose to follow them?

Continue at Home

1. Write on a note card all the Scriptures that ministered to you in this chapter. Use them to help you apply these principles.

2. Conduct an experiment: Watch for incidents this week where you experience being Chart 12 (single-minded), showing forth God and walking after His Spirit. Also note the times when you are Chart 13. Picture these charts in your mind.

3. Ask God this week to make you aware of the times when you make emotional choices to follow your own thoughts and emotions, over what He is prompting you to do. When He shows you something, stop, pray, identify the problem, confess it, repent of it, give it to God and then get into His Word. Watch for examples that you might share with the group.

4. Ask God to show you the things you have been burying and not dealing with (things that are blocking you from experiencing His Life through you). When He reveals these things to you, praise Him and then "deal with them" the proper way.

MEMORIZE: **READ:**
Ephesians 3:19   Galatians 5:24-25
Luke 11:33   Ephesians 6:5-6
2 Corinthians 4:10-11   1 Kings 8:10-11

Chapter 11: The Hidden Chambers
(Part 1)

Overview

The hidden chambers of the temple were a part of the upper level of the Inner Court and were built all around the outside of the sanctuary. These chambers were supposed to be used for storing the priest's items of worship. However, because these chambers were "hidden and secret," the priests stored their own personal, idolatrous worship items there, thinking "no one will see and no one will know."

These secret recesses, I believe, correspond to our subconscious, the place in our soul where we, too, hide and bury our hurts, wounds, insecurities, etc., thinking "no one will see and no one will know." Scripture tells us that these chambers can often become "chambers of death" because many of us don't know how to allow God to expose, cleanse and heal them. Every time we don't deal with our sin the proper way but simply bury it, we give Satan access to these chambers. So, these buried things do influence us, but they don't need to determine our choices and thus our actions.

God allows the power of sin access into this area as a means of exposing what's down there. He wants us to see for ourselves what's there and then choose to give these things over to Him, so that His Life from our hearts can come forth instead. Unless we see these hidden things, we won't know what to give over to Him.

So as Christians, God wants us to stop burying and pushing down our "real" feelings. He wants us to allow His Holy Spirit to expose the truth so that He can truly heal us. Only God can take away these hidden things "as far as the east is from the west." Then, once the root cause of our sin has been exposed and gotten rid of, then the surface symptoms will not occur again either.

Group Discussion Questions

1. What was the original purpose of the *hidden chambers* of Solomon's Temple? (2 Chronicles 31:11-12; Nehemiah 13:4-5) What was actually stored there? (Ezekiel 8:6-12)

2. Why do you think these *hidden chambers* are so significant? (1 Chronicles 28:11-12; 1 Kings 6:5-13)

3. What do these hidden chambers correspond to in us? (Proverbs 18:8; Ezekiel 8:12)

4. Do you believe Satan can read our thoughts? (2 Corinthians 2:10-11; Ephesians 4:26-27; John 14:30)

5. Can a Christian be "demon-possessed"? (Colossians 1:12-15; 1 John 5:18; John 10:27-29)

6. What is a good definition of our subconscious?

7. What is it that triggers our self-life? (Nehemiah 4:10) Why?

8. Why does God allow the *power of sin* access to these hidden chambers? (Deuteronomy 7:20; Psalm 51:6)

9. Why is it important that we "see" these hidden things? (Jeremiah 1:10)

10. What exactly does God mean when He says, in Matthew 16:24, that we are to "deny ourselves?" Does this mean to hide and bury our real feelings? Why/Why not?

11. Why is it that many people who have gone through counseling often "end up worse off than when they first began"? (Isaiah 30:1; Jeremiah 30:12)

12. Why is it so important to ask God to reveal the hidden *root causes* of our negative thoughts and emotions? (Proverbs 3:19-20)

Personal Questions

1. What key points in this chapter stood out to you or have affected you the most?

2. Have you or are you struggling with any similar situations to those that were shared in this chapter?

3. In your own life, can you think of some examples of things that triggered your hidden "self-life"? How did you handle these things? Has God given you some new tools to use through this study?

4. Can you think of some situations or examples where you believe Satan did read you thoughts? How did you handle it? How did you give it to God?

5. Have you ever given things over to God and then felt like they returned? What did you end up doing? Has God revealed new truths to you in this area? What things?

6. Does the temple model help you in understanding how a Christian cannot be demon-possessed?

7. Is this teaching about the hidden chambers new for you? Does it help in explaining some of your own actions?

8. 8. Do you ever bury and stuff your real feelings thinking that "something is wrong with you" or that "you are a bad person"? What happened? What are we allowing Satan to do when we choose not to deal with our hidden hurts, fears and insecurities?

9. Why are the *hidden chambers* often called "chambers of death"? What does God desire for these chambers? What do you act out of, if you haven't dealt with the "hidden things" that God is trying to bring up?

10. Why does Satan want you to bury and stuff your negative thoughts and feelings? If we have buried things in the past, should we try and search out these things ourselves? Why/ why not?

Continue at Home

1. Write on a note card all the Scriptures that particularly ministered to you in this chapter. Use them to help you apply these principles.

2. Watch yourself this week and if you "over-react" to circumstances or something someone said, stop and ask God to show you what the *root cause* really is. When He does, write it down and choose to give it over to God. Be sure to "reprogram" God's Truth back in where the lies have been, so that more lies don't return.

3. Pray and ask God to show you other things that you have been stuffing in your hidden chambers. Deal with these things the proper way and by faith, believe that God has cleansed you. Don't allow these things to come back again by continually thinking about them and meditating on them.

4. This week, ask God to show you any lies about yourself that you have programmed in over the years and upon which you are basing your choices. Choose to give these things over to God and again, replace them with His Truth. (See the *Knowing God Loves Me* Scriptures in the back of the textbook.)

5. Write down any areas that you are still struggling with, either with yourself or in this teaching. Bring them before the Lord daily.

MEMORIZE:	**READ:**
Psalm 51:6	Romans 7:20-21
Matthew 16:24	John 10:27-29
John 8:32	Nehemiah 4:10-11
1 John 5:18	
Colossians 1:13-14	

Chapter 12: The Hidden Chambers
(Part 2)

Overview

The "freeing" that we have been talking about in *Be Ye Transformed* is a process—a process of healing. And, it's a process that we will be in until we see Jesus. This "freeing" is dependent upon our moment-by-moment choices and God's faithfulness.

We must trust God completely, knowing that it is His Will for us to be free. Only God knows everything that needs to be dealt with in our hidden chambers, and only He can heal us completely of these things. Our friends, professionals, counselors and pastors cannot deal with our sin. We must do that for ourselves. God will expose our sins; we must then confess and repent of them, and allow Him to cleanse us completely from them.

Christ wants us to die to our self-life—to set it aside, to deny it and to surrender it—so that He can live His Life through us. So as Christians, we don't have to "work at" cleaning up our past, but simply give God permission to expose the real "root causes" of our present problems.

If we try to analyze and figure out our past for ourselves, we will simply reprogram those negative thoughts and emotions right back down in our hidden chambers, and then they will become even stronger strongholds.

God is the only One who, by His Spirit, can reveal the hidden causes for our hurts today. If, however, we don't realize the authority and power we possess through the Mind of Christ, we never will truly be free of our past.

Group Discussion Questions

1. Define "deliverance" as we have been using the term in this study. (Romans 6:11) Is there a need for deliverance from demons for Christians? Why/ why not?

2. Can we cleanse all of the things in our hidden chambers all at once? Why/ why not?

3. Should we be afraid of what God might bring up from the hidden chambers that we must deal with or afraid of how and when He might bring them up? (2 Timothy 1:7)

4. What does the word, *psychology* mean? How is the way of psychology any different from the way the Bible teaches? (2 Corinthians 4:11-12)

5. Psychology teaches us to blame others for not loving us perfectly. What does this way of thinking do to us? What does the Bible teach?

6. Why can psychology actually become dangerous to our souls? (Philippians 3:13)

7. Psychology teaches us to make an appointment with a counselor and then, in their timing we try and figure out (often by visualization) our past by looking for the hidden things. What does the Bible teach? (2 Corinthians 10:5)

8. Do we need to be healed from all the "garbage" of the past in order to make faith choices? Why/ why not?

9. Why is it so important to put the *truth* of God's Word back into our hidden chambers after He has freed us from strongholds there? (Luke 11:24-26)

Personal Questions

1. What key points of this chapter stood out to you or has affected your life the most and why?

2. Can you think of a place in your life right now where you might be able to apply these principles? If so, what areas?

3. What are you allowing Satan to do when you choose not to "deal with" what God is trying to show you from your hidden chambers?

4. Is there any area of your life right now where you cannot change the circumstances, but need to be *released* from the bondage of your emotions concerning this situation?

5. How can we become free from our hurts, fears, insecurities, guilt, etc.? Is this a one-time occurrence? Why/ why not?

6. Once our hidden chambers are cleansed and emptied, can they be re-filled with junk again?

7. Have you ever blamed others for not loving you perfectly? What happened? Are you freed now?

8.   Is it a new concept to you, to make sure you put God's Word back in your "hidden chambers" after you have made a faith choice? What did you do before? Did it work?

Continue at Home

1.   Write on a note card all the Scriptures that particularly ministered to you in this chapter. Use them to help you apply these principles.

2.   This week be particularly sensitive to "taking every (negative or ungodly) thought captive" and "revenging all disobedience" (deal with your sin). Note in your journal as you experience the chain-reaction of your soul. Confess the wrong choices as sin, and then deal with these thoughts and feelings as God would have you.

3.   Ask God to show you if you are hanging on to any hurts, doubts, fears, pride, resentments ("justified" or not) that might be blocking you from experiencing His Life in your soul.

4.   Think of a person who triggers ungodly reactions in you. Pray and ask God to show you the *root cause* of these feelings. When God shows you, then "deal with" those emotions the way God would have you. (Psalm 139:22-24)

5.   Write down what God is showing you personally about cleansing the hidden chambers. What are some specific things that He is speaking directly to you about?

MEMORIZE: **READ:**
Matthew 7:14   2 Peter 2:20
2 Corinthians 10:5-6   James 1:3-4
Romans 14:23   Luke 11:24-26
Proverbs 3:20

Chapter 13: How God's Mind Works in Us

Overview

We have seen that Solomon's Temple represents the internal architecture of a man indwelt by the Holy Spirit. The floorplan of the Temple is a perfect blueprint of a believer—spirit, heart, will and soul.

Therefore, if the architecture of Solomon's Temple holds such significance to us as believers, then I surmise that the features and the furnishings of the Temple must have just as much meaning. I believe they represent the different facets of the seven-fold Spirit of God that produces the Mind of Christ in us.

By studying these features and furnishings in depth, we'll understand a little more clearly just how God's Spirit equips us to walk in intimate knowledge of God and fear Him only. The details of the furniture, and the rituals surrounding them, become the Scriptural basis for the practical application steps of renewing our minds that we will explore in the next chapter.

To be "renewed in the Spirit of our minds" means *putting off* our own self-centered and ungodly thoughts and emotions and *putting on* the Mind of Christ. It means putting on God's Wisdom, His Understanding, His Counsel, His Strength, walking in intimate Knowledge of Him and Fearing Him only.

Group Discussion Questions

1. What do the features and furnishings of the Temple represent?

2. We mentioned in Chapter Nine that the Holy of Holies represented the *new spirit* we receive as a result of being born again. What are the three features or furnishings of the Holy of Holies and what do they represent symbolically in us? (Psalm 99:1; John 14:23; 1 Kings 8:29)

3. There were also three pieces of furniture in the Holy Place. What were they and what was each of their functions? (1 Kings 7:48-49; 2 Chronicles 4:19-20)

4. What does the Altar of Incense represent in us and why is it so special? What room was this Altar really a part of? (Hebrews 9:3-4)

5. Where are the three places that God promises "to meet with us"? What do these places represent? (Exodus 25:21-22; 30:1-6; 29:38-42)

6. What exactly is the *new life* that God creates in our hearts? (Romans 5:5; Luke 8:12; Isaiah 11:2) Of that new Life, what is it that makes up the Mind of Christ?

7. The fire on the Golden Altar of Incense was kept perpetually burning. What does this symbolize for us? How did the priests keep it continuously burning? (Hebrews 10:10-14)

8. In review what are the three pieces of furniture in the Holy Place and what part of the Mind of Christ in us do they represent?

9. The Porch represents our new willpower. What are the two separate areas of the temple porch? What was their purpose and what do they represent in us? (Zechariah 4:11-12)

10. What do the upper and lower levels of the Inner Court represent of the Mind of Christ in us? Explain this function of the Mind of Christ.

11. What is so special about the last two functions of the Mind of Christ in us? (Philippians 2:12)

12. Name the three features of the Inner Court and, as best you can, tell the order of service for the priests. After the Inner Court Ritual, what did they do?

13. What do the three pieces of furniture in the Inner Court represent in us? (2 Corinthians 7:1; Hosea 6:6)

14. God tells us in 1 John 5:8 that there are three cleansing agents at work in our souls. What are they and what do they do for us? Correlate these to the three pieces of furniture in the Inner Court.

15. Read John 13:7-10 and describe what you see Jesus saying here. (1 John 1: 9)

16. Why is forgiveness such an important part of our confession and repentance? (Matthew 6:14-15; John 13:14)

17. The Holocaust Altar is where we show our love to God. Can you explain this? (Ephesians 5:2; Hosea 6:6)

18. What did the priests do at the Molten Sea? What is this symbolic of and why? (Ephesians 5:26; Psalms 107:20)

19. In your own words, what are the three steps we must take to cleanse our souls (our feet)? (1 John 5:8; Revelation 12:11; Ephesians 4:22-24) If we do this, what do we receive in exchange? (John 12:24-25; 2 Corinthians 4:11)

Personal Questions

1. What key points of the chapter stood out to you and/ or have affected your life the most and why?

2. Can you think of an example in your own life where you might be able to apply this teaching?

3. Our responsibility is to choose to hand over to God "anything that is not of faith." Name some of the common sins (like criticalness, judgmentalness) that plague you and quench God's Life in you, just as much as the "big" sins of Galatians 5.

4. What will we receive as a result of totally giving ourselves over to God? (2 Corinthians 2:14; 4:11)

5. Can we eventually reach a plateau in our walk with God where we can simply coast for awhile and not have to make, moment-by-moment faith choices? Why/ why not?

6. Has learning about the priest's order of service in the Inner Court given you any new insights about your own daily walk with God? If so, in what ways?

7. Why is it so crucial to "wash yourself" of negative thoughts, emotions and desires, even if they are "justified" by the world's standards?

8. How does sacrificing and giving over to God "anything that is not of faith" show our love for God?

Continue at Home

1. Write on a note card all the Scriptures that particularly ministered to you in this chapter. Use them to help you apply these principles.

2. In this chapter, which Temple furniture, feature or ritual impacted or interested you the most? Why? Write your answer in your journal. Be prepared to share.

3. Begin this week to *confess and repent* of anything "that is not of faith" and unconditionally *forgive* anyone who has wronged you; be sure to then *give over to God* all that He has shown you; and, don't forget to jump into His Word and replace the lies with the Truth.

4. Write on a 3x5 note card the "Forgiveness" Scriptures in the back of this book. Pick the ones that particularly minister to you and memorize them.

MEMORIZE:
Ephesians 5:26
1 John 1:9
Matthew 7:14
Hosea 6:6
Zechariah 4:11-12

READ:
John 13:7-10, 14
Luke 11:39-41
Hebrews 9:3-5
Hebrews 10:12-14

Chapter 14: How Do We Renew Our Minds?
(Attitudes)

Overview

As we daily renew our minds, there are four *attitudes* that are essential to have in order to be transformed. First of all, we must have an attitude of being willing to daily present our bodies to God as a living sacrifice. In order to do this, we must know that God loves us unconditionally. Only then can we willingly, without reservation, give Him permission to expose anything in us that is "not of faith."

Next, we must be willing to daily deny ourselves—to yield, surrender and relinquish to God all our rights, frustrations, etc. Each of us must be willing to give over to God all our thoughts, emotions and desires that are contrary to His. Every Christian is "capable" of doing this (because God is in them), however, only a few are willing to do this in action. In order to be transformed the way God desires, we must not only be willing to give over our self-life (inside) to God, we must also be willing to get up and *do* (on the outside) whatever it is that God has asked us to do. No matter how we feel, what we think or what we want, we must willingly take that next step of action.

Finally, we must be willing to "take every thought captive" and be ready to "revenge all disobedience." If we don't catch our negative thoughts, we'll end up going along with the tide of emotion and quenching God's Spirit. Remember, God's Voice is always in perfect agreement with His Word. Any voice that does not corroborate with God's Word is not His Voice at all. Therefore, it's crucial to be aware of, recognize and catch any thoughts that are not from God. We are to refuse them, crucify them and give them to God.

Group Discussion Questions

1. What are the four *attitudes* we must constantly have in order to be "transformed" the way God desires? (Romans 12:1-2; Philippians 3:8-15; Philippians 2:5-8; 2 Corinthians 10:5-6) Do we need to "feel" each of these attitudes? Why/why not? (Romans 1:17)

2.   Romans 12:1 tells us we are to "present [our] bodies [as] a living sacrifice."
      What does this mean to you? (Job 13:15; 2 Corinthians 7:1; 2 Timothy 2:
      21)

3.   As we open ourselves up to God, what basic fact must we always remember?
      (1 John 4:10; Jeremiah 31:3)

4.   When we talk about "denying ourselves," what exactly do we mean?
      (Philippians 3:8-15; John 12:24; Colossians 3:5, 8-9) Are all Christians
      capable of denying themselves and laying everything down? If so, why
      aren't more of them doing so?

5.   Another critical attitude we must have on, is that of *being willing to do*
      what God has asked us to do. How does this differ from the second step of
      "denying ourselves"? (2 Corinthians 8:11; Matthew 26:39; Luke 5:5)

6.   Summarize why it's so important to "take every thought captive." (2
      Corinthians 10:5-6) Is our first negative thought sin? Why/ why not? (2
      Samuel 11:2-4)

7.   Can you briefly explain the differences between God's Thoughts and the
      thoughts that Satan and self interject in our souls? (1 Kings 19:12; James 1:
      13-15; Genesis 3:1)

8.   If we have confessed, repented and given our negative thoughts over to God and they still won't go away, what should we do? (2 Corinthians 10:3-4)

9.   If responsible for the original negative thought when it first comes in, where does the sin occur? (Romans 7:15-17; 2 Corinthians 10:5; Philippians 4:8) Why? What happens if we choose to do nothing with those thoughts?

Personal Questions

1.   What key points of this chapter stood out the most to you and why?

2.   Have you or are you struggling with any situation similar to those that were shared in this chapter? If so, what situations?

3.   What do you "naturally" tend to do with your negative thoughts and feelings? Give examples. What does God desire that you do? Are you willing to do this?

4.   What things tend to quench God's Spirit in your life? Is there a situation in your life right now where you feel "justified" in holding onto your negative thoughts? What are you allowing Satan to do in the meantime?

5.   Have you in the past given things over to God and had them return? What have you learned about this that might help you in the future?

6. What are some of the thoughts Satan usually interjects into your thinking? What do you do with these things? Have you made it a habit to "take every thought captive"? Has it changed or helped your walk with God now?

7. When you "denied yourself" before, did you just think it meant *bury your real feelings*?

8. In the past, have you been afraid to "open" yourself up to God? Why? What are you basically afraid of?

Continue at Home

1. Write on a note card all the Scriptures that particularly ministered to you in this chapter. Use them to help you apply these principles.

2. In your journal, describe what self-centered thoughts, emotions and desires get in your way of being transformed. Write these down and then give them to God by confessing them, repenting of them and getting in His Word.

3. This week, be aware of any thinking that takes your peace away. Ask God to show you specifically what is quenching His Spirit and causing the separation. Note in your journal the things God tells you and the things you give over to Him. Also, note the Scriptures He gives you to replace the lies and the untruths.

4. Again, be sure and read over the *Knowing God Loves Me* Scriptures in the back of this workbook. Put the ones that particularly minister to you on 3x5 note cards and memorize them.

MEMORIZE:	**READ:**
Romans 12:1; 8:6	Philippians 3:8-15
Job 13:15	Philippians 2:5-9
Philippians 4:8	2 Corinthians 10:3-5
Matthew 26:39	Psalm 139:23-24
Luke 5:5	

Chapter 15: How Do We Renew Our Minds?
(Inner Court Ritual)

Overview

In the last chapter we focused on the four attitudes that we need to have in order to be "renewed in the spirit of our minds." In this chapter we explore the four *mandatory steps* (the Inner Court Ritual) that we must take each time we find that we have quenched God's Spirit. These are the practical steps to how we "revenge all disobedience."

These four steps were the actual ritual that the priests of Solomon's Temple went through in the Inner Court in order to deal with their sin. Going through these steps every time we are confronted with a hurtful remark, a painful situation, pride, fear and so on is the only way we can stay cleansed and prepared vessels for what God might call us to do next.

The first thing we must do in order to "deal with our sin" is to acknowledge and experience our real negative thoughts and emotions (our self-life) as they occur. It's imperative to recognize what we are thinking and feeling and to call it for what it is. Then, we'll know exactly what to give over to the Lord. We can't give things over to Him if we don't really know what they are.

The next step of the Inner Court Ritual is to confess and repent of all that the Holy Spirit has shown us, and by faith forgive anyone who has wronged us. Once God has shown us our own sin and we have confessed it and repented of it, it's imperative at that point to give that sin over to the Lord. Finally, we must read God's Word and replace the lies with the truth. God is the only One who can cleanse us, sanctify us and heal us completely by His Word.

This is how the Inner Court Ritual works. And this is what we must do moment-by-moment in order to renew our minds and be transformed into Christ's image. It's our own responsibility to *put off* the old man and to *put on* Christ. We already possess God's Life in our hearts (if we are born again), we just must make sure that's what's showing forth in our lives.

Group Discussion Questions

1. What is the difference between the four *attitudes* of the last chapter and the *Inner Court Ritual*? (Romans 8:6; 2 Corinthians 10:6)

2. What are the four *mandatory* steps (the Inner Court Ritual) that the Old Testament has laid out for us? (Proverbs 20:27; 2 Corinthians 13:5; Job 12:22; Proverbs 1:23; 1 John 1:9; Acts 8:22; Matthew 6:14-15; Colossians 3:5, 8; Ephesians 5:26; John 15:3)

3. Why is it important to recognize the negative thoughts and emotions that we are experiencing? Wouldn't it just be simpler to vent these things or bury them? Why/ why not? (2 Corinthians 13:5; Psalms 139:23-24)

4. Why is it so critical to be a cleansed vessel when "taking a stand" with someone?

5. Why is it so important to ask God to expose the "root cause" of our thoughts and feelings? (Proverbs 5:22; Job 12:22) Why do we need to "see" these buried things? (Psalm 139:23-24)

6. As Christians, we have three choices as to what we can do with our negative thoughts and feelings. What are they? What is the best way of dealing with these things? (Psalm 103:12)

7. Do the things we push down in our hidden chambers stay there, or do they affect our lives in some way? What do we enable Satan to do when we don't deal with the negative things in our hidden chambers? (Proverbs 5:22; John 8:34)

8. Define *confession* and *repentance*. (Isaiah 1:16; Ezekiel 18:30; 1 John 1:9)

9. Who is responsible for changing our feelings? Can't we just pray harder and change our own feelings?

10. If someone has offended us, do we wait to forgive him until he comes to us and asks? (Matthew 6:14-15; 18:32-35; Colossians 3:13) What if we are "justified" feeling the way we do?

11. What are the two steps involved in forgiveness? (Matthew 18:35; 2 Corinthians 2:10)

12. In your own words, what does it mean to *give over to God* (sacrifice) all that He has shown us about ourselves? (Luke 11:39-40; 1 Peter 5:7; Ephesians 5: 2; 2 Timothy 2:21) Give examples from your own life.

13. Why is it so important to "get into the Word" after we have given everything over to the Lord? Explain. (Luke 11:24-26; Ephesians 5:26; John 15:3; James 1:21)

14. After we have completed the Inner Court Ritual, what are some other very important things we should do?

Personal Questions

1. What key points in this chapter stood out the most to you and why?

2. Have you or are you experiencing any situations or struggles similar to those that were shared in this chapter? If so, what situations?

3. If you minister to someone, what *attitude* is critical for you to have *before* you can exhort them or recite Scripture to them? Do you have any examples of this in your own life? Open discussion.

4. Have you ever waited for someone to come to you and ask forgiveness? What happened? Did they ever come? What happened to you in the meantime?

5. Have you learned anything different about giving things over to God? What specifics have you learned that are new?

6. In the past, were you as aware of your sin as you are now? Did you confess it and repent of it, or did you just give it to God? What is different, if anything? How are you handling it now?

7. Have you ever tried to change you own feelings before? What happened?
    What are you doing now?

8. If we hear something bad about a Christian brother or sister, what is the best
    way of handling the situation? Why? (Proverbs 17:17; Ephesians 4:15)

Continue at Home

1. Write out the Inner Court Ritual for yourself. Write the steps on 3x5 cards
    and keep these cards with you at all times. You will need them when you are
    away from your notebook and your Bible. This week, every time you find
    yourself over-reacting to someone or something, or losing your peace, pull
    out the cards and go through the steps of cleansing.

2. Be sure you are keeping up your consistent quiet time before the Lord. It's
    in our times before the Lord that we are able to give over to God all of our
    negative thoughts and emotions and go through the Inner Court Ritual. It's
    critical to do this, so that we are "ready and prepared" to handle whatever
    God allows in our lives next. If we don't have our quiet times to get clean,
    we'll contaminate everyone we come in contact with.

3. Write a love letter to God and give Him permission to expose all your hurts,
    anger, unforgiveness, etc. Remember, He loves you and wants you free. Ask
    Him to reveal areas of pride, unbelief and any other strongholds of the enemy.
    Then allow Him to do so.

4. Ask God to make you more aware this week of any negative thoughts you
    might have towards others. When He shows you, immediately give these
    thoughts over to Him and go through the Inner Court Ritual. Make this a
    habit in your life.

MEMORIZE
James 4:7
2 Corinthians 10:6
Ephesians 4:15
Psalm 103:12
Ephesians 5:26
Romans 8:28
Hebrew 10:22

READ:
Mark 11:25-26
Luke 11:39-41

Chapter 16: Results of a Renewed Mind

Overview

There are many results of a renewed mind. Here are just a few.

After we have been "renewed in the spirit of our minds," God promises in His Word that we can come boldly to the throne of God and present our love offerings. He says these offerings are now acceptable to Him because they are things done in His righteousness and not our own.

Another result of a renewed mind is that we will become true worshippers of God, who "worship Him in spirit and in truth." These are the ones who bring the Love that God originally placed in their hearts when they were first born again, full circle back to Him now as a love offering. At this point, we can be assured that God will hear our prayers because they are now according to His Will and not our own.

All the facets of the Mind of Christ will be operating in us: His Wisdom and Understanding, His Counsel and Strength. We will be experiencing intimate Knowledge of God and walking in Fear of Him. At this point, we will begin to see all that happens to us from His perspective and won't be buried in our own emotions. Also, we'll have on the *full* armor of God, which is the only way, Scripture tells us, that we will ever be able to stand in the battle against the enemy of our souls.

Jesus' Life is the *light of men* and this is the Life that He wants shining and beaming through each of us. The question is: Will He see your light? Will you be ready and prepared to go with Him? Will He know You intimately?

Group Discussion Questions

1.   Name some of the *results* of a renewed mind.

2. Explain why our offerings are acceptable to God, once we have gone through the Inner Court Ritual and have been cleansed. Why not before? (Malachi 3: 3; Psalm 4:5)

3. John 4:23-24 tells us that the true worshippers of God are those who worship Him in Spirit and in Truth. What does this mean to you? (Psalm 29:2)

4. One of the most wonderful results of a renewed mind is that we can be assured God will now hear our own prayers. (1 John 5:14-15)

5. Name all the facets of the Mind of Christ that become available to us, when we renew our minds. (Isaiah 11:1-2)

6. At this point, God promises us, whether we feel like it or not, that our lives have been *transformed*. What does this really mean? (Ephesians 3:19; Galatians 2:20)

7. When our minds are renewed, we'll be able to "see" all that happens to us from God's perspective. Why is this so critical? (Genesis 50:20)

8. One of the most important results of a renewed mind is that we will have on the full armor of God—His armor of Light. (Ephesians 6:13-19; Romans 13: 12-14) As best you can, describe each piece of armor and what it does.

Personal Questions

1. What key points stood out to you in this chapter the most and why?

2. Are there any areas in your life right now where you might be able to apply this teaching? If so, what areas?

3. Man's wisdom will lead you to be conformed into the _____ image. Whereas, God's Wisdom will lead you to be conformed into _____ _____ Image.

4. Renewing your mind gives you the ability to do what? How does this relate to your *purpose* as a Christian?

5. What is your own responsibility in renewing your mind?

6. As a result of these principles being applied to your life over the last few weeks, do you see your life changing and becoming more transformed? In what ways?

7. Are there any areas of your life where you can see that you are "living the truth" where perhaps you weren't before? What areas?

Continue for the Rest of Your Life

1. Don't put this study on a shelf and forget it. Continually keep *Be Ye Transformed* foremost in your mind. Keep reading the book and listening to the tapes. Constantly renew your thinking in order that you might stay an open channel, receiving God's Life and then being a vessel to pass it on.

2. Ask God to continue to show you the areas in your life where you are still not "living the truth." As He reveals these areas to you, go through the steps to renewing your mind. Stay that cleansed and open vessel before Him in Love.

3. Continue to practice the Inner Court Ritual daily. Keep your cards with those four steps close at hand. So many have their lives changed as a result of learning these principles of God, but once the study is over, they go back to their old ways. Don't let that happen to you. Continue to "*Be Transformed* by the renewing of your mind."

4. Keep your precious quiet time before the Lord. Read His Word daily. Let Him continue to show you the root causes of your negative thoughts and emotions; continue being cleansed, changed and transformed into His Image.

5. Continue your journal. It's a wonderful way of documenting your adventure with God and of being able to review all that He has done for you.

"Be not conformed to this world, but *be ye transformed* (how?) by the renewing of your mind, that ye may prove what is the good, and acceptable, and perfect, will of God." (Romans 12:1-2)

Role of the Discussion Leader

Your role as a leader is simply to stimulate discussion by asking the appropriate questions and encouraging people to respond.

Your leadership is a gift to the other members of the group. Keep in mind that they, too, share responsibility for the group. If you are nervous, realize you are not the first to feel this way. Many Biblical leaders—Moses, Joshua, and even the apostle Paul—felt nervous and inadequate to lead others.

Leader Objectives

The following are suggested objectives to help you become an effective leader.

- To guide the discussion, to clarify understanding, and to keep the group focused on the lesson.

- To steer the group into a meaningful exchange among themselves.

- To help the participants learn from each other.

- To keep the group discussion focused on the key points found in the *Scriptural Reference Outlines* at the end of each chapter.

- To be a neutral person leading the discussion back to Scripture and the key points if it wanders.

- To assist the group in finding practical applications for the principles discussed.

- To encourage each person to participate in the group discussion.

- To make the discussion group a non-threatening place for all to share their ideas.

- To have a positive attitude and to provide encouragement to the group.

- To guide, rather than dominate, the discussion.

Preparing to Lead

First of all, it's critical that you, the leader of the discussion group, be a cleansed vessel filled with God's Love and Wisdom—a "living example" of someone who has been transformed. This message must first be applied to your own life. Otherwise, you will not be genuinely prepared to lead others. You must have a working knowledge of the *Be Ye Transformed* principles, so you can share what God has done in your own life. You cannot "give out" something you have never "experienced" for yourself.

Only by being real and transparent yourself, sharing your own failures as well as your victories, will genuineness ever be brought into the discussion. It's important to remember that you *don't have to be "perfect" in order to guide a discussion, you simply must be an open vessel pointing others to the only One who is perfect—and that's Jesus.*

Paramount to any Bible study is prayer. Be sure to pray for the group before and after each study and do much private prayer during the discussion itself. Pray for each member of the group during the week, always remembering that prayer is the only thing that unleashes the power of God to work in all our lives.

Read the assigned chapter in the *Be Ye Transformed* textbook. Answer each question in the corresponding chapter in the workbook. Meditate and reflect upon each passage of Scripture as you formulate your answers.

Familiarize yourself with the Scriptural Reference Outlines at the end of each chapter in the textbook. These will help you understand the important points to make in the discussion and provide more information about the questions.

You might also want to purchase the *Be Ye Transformed Leader's Guide* containing "suggested" answers for each question. There are no "right" answers; these are just suggestions. Be sure to allow the Holy Spirit room to answer the questions the way He desires.

As a leader, you must be a sensitive listener, not only to the members of the group but also to the Holy Spirit. As you ask the appropriate questions, allow the Holy Spirit to direct your responses and give you discernment as to who needs a special touch (a hug, an encouragement, time afterwards, etc.).

Remember, as the leader of the discussion, you are simply a channel God is using to stimulate and guide the conversation—the Holy Spirit is always the teacher. Do <u>not</u> do all the talking, but involve every member of the group, always seeing that the sharing is edifying and pointed towards Jesus.

Leading the Study

Always begin the study on time. If everyone realizes that you begin on time, the members of the group will make a greater effort to be there on time—they won't want to miss anything.

At the beginning of your first meeting, you might share that these studies are designed to be discussions, not lectures. Encourage everyone to participate.

The discussion questions in the workbook are designed to be used just as they are written. If you wish, you may read each one aloud to the group. Or you may prefer to express them in your own words. However, unnecessary rewording of the questions is not recommended.

Don't be afraid of silence. People in the group need time to think before responding.

Try to avoid answering your own questions. If necessary, keep rephrasing a question until it is clearly understood. If the group thinks you will always answer for them, they will keep silent.

Encourage more than one answer to each question. You might ask, "What do the rest of you think?" or "Anyone else?" Allow several people to respond.

Never reject an answer. Be as affirming as possible. If a person's answer is clearly wrong, you might ask, "What lead you to that conclusion?" Or let the group handle the problem by asking them what they think about the question.

Avoid going off on tangents. If people wander off course, gently bring them back to the question at hand.

Try to end on time. This is often difficult to do, but if you control the pace of the discussion by not spending too much time on some questions, you should be able to finish at the appropriate time. A discussion group of about 45 minutes to an hour is perfect.

Additional Suggestions for Leaders

Besides being that open and cleansed vessel and constantly praying, there are several other *skills* that you, as the leader of the discussion, should pray about developing:

Pray for and develop *good communication skills.* Communication will not only be your words, but also your "body language." Even though someone might share something shocking in the discussion, be careful not to offend the participant by your response. Acknowledge the person, yet all the while asking God for *His* response to what they have just shared. Be confident that God will give you the Love you need and also the Wisdom you need to respond "wisely in Love."

Try to really understand what the participant is sharing. If necessary, repeat what you think he/she is saying. For example, you might ask: "Is this what you are saying..." or, "You mean...?"

Another very important asset for you, as the leader of the group, to acquire is to be a *good listener.* Everyone is desperate for someone to listen to them, especially when they are going through critical emotional issues. Whenever someone is talking, give them your undivided attention. Your eyes should be on the person sharing and you should try to acknowledge them as much as you can (again, always praying silently to God for His response).

Another vital skill to develop is to *be an encourager.* Set an example for your group by encouraging the members continually. Without encouragement, your sharing times will be nothing more than answering homework questions at school. (You might even suggest that the following week, each of the members of the group phone and encourage someone else in the group.)

One of the most difficult tasks that you will face is *how to keep one person from dominating* the group. You need to allow each person in the group an opportunity to share, but you must prevent any *one* person from doing all the talking (including yourself). One member of the group who continually dominates the discussion can derail and quench an otherwise anointed sharing time. You mustn't rush the person speaking, giving the Holy Spirit ample time to minister and guide the discussion, but at the same time you are responsible to keep the discussion on target and to accomplish all that needs to be done.

A few suggestions to prevent one person dominating the discussion:

- You might interrupt the particular person speaking and restate what you have just heard him/her say.

- You might repeat the question you previously asked the group. The dominating person might be startled at first by the interruption, but should respond by answering the second question more directly.

- If this does not work, then you should ask the participant to please let the other group members share their views also.

Another invaluable skill for you, as the leader of the discussion, to have is knowing how to *involve all the members* of the group in the discussion. Discussion groups are not for lecturing—each individual must be encouraged to interact. Ideally, everyone should have an opportunity to share. Ask open-ended questions to specific individuals, especially ones that are reluctant to volunteer anything themselves.

Again, it's important not to criticize, make fun of, or put anyone down. Remember, be an encourager. Learn how to correct a group member's answer in a positive way and then, as tactfully as you can, go on to the next person.

Helpful Hints for Leaders

Always open the discussion with prayer and close the session with prayer. Pray that God will help each of you to apply the Biblical principles daily.

Start out the first session by sharing a little about yourself. How has *Be Ye Transformed* affected or changed your life? Go around the circle and have each member share five minutes about himself/herself.

In the succeeding meetings, begin each session by asking:

- "Which key points stood out to you during this session?"

- "Which points challenged you or encouraged you?"

- "Could any of you relate to some of the situations or struggles that were shared in this chapter?

- "Are any of you experiencing similar situations?"

- "In what areas of your life might you be able to apply this teaching?"

Suggest that each member of the group during the week write down any questions they may have while reading the textbook, listening to the tapes or watching the video, so they can talk about them during the group discussion.

Lean heavily on the Scriptural Reference Outlines at the end of each chapter for the *key points* to emphasize.

Reproduce **Charts 1-25** in the *Be Ye Transformed* textbook and post them in each of the appropriate sessions, so the group can constantly refer to them.

Finally, stress complete confidentiality. Set an example for the group by being the first to be trustworthy.

"No man, when he hath lighted a candle, putteth it in a
secret place, neither under a bushel, but on a candlestick,
that they which come in may see the light.

The light of the body is the eye; therefore when thine eye
is single, thy whole body also is full of light; but when
thine eye is evil, thy body also is full of darkness.

Take heed therefore that the light which is in thee be not
darkness."

Luke 11:33-35

Personal Notes

Personal Notes

Personal Notes

Personal Notes

Personal Notes

Personal Notes

Personal Notes

Personal Notes

Personal Notes

Personal Notes

Personal Notes

Personal Notes

Personal Notes

Personal Notes